WHEN YOUR LIFE INCLUDES A WHEELCHAIR

By
MARILYN MURRAY WILLISON

Desert Ministries, Inc.
Matthews, North Carolina

ALSO BY MARILYN MURRAY WILLISON

DIARY OF A DIVORCED MOTHER
TIME ENOUGH FOR LOVE
THE SELF-CONFIDENCE TRICK

WHEN YOUR LIFE INCLUDES A WHEELCHAIR

First Edition
©Copyright 2004 by
Desert Ministries, Inc.
P.O. Box 747
Matthews, North Carolina 28106-0747
ISBN 0-914733-31-1

Printed by Eagle Graphic Services, Fort Lauderdale, Florida

DEDICATION

FOR TONY FRAGIACOMO
MY BELOVED HUSBAND

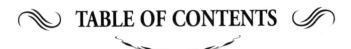

TABLE OF CONTENTS

INTRODUCTION

By Ginny Thornburgh

Dear Reader,

I happily write this introduction to Marilyn Willison's book, *When Your Life Includes A Wheelchair* and commend it to you as a gift from an author who knows, understands and lives with multiple sclerosis. Her book reveals the wonderful and talented woman Marilyn is: open, honest and optimistic.

I am familiar with disability from the perspective of a parent. My husband Dick and I have an adult son Peter whose mental retardation was caused by an automobile accident when he was only four months old. Although quite limited, Peter today is able to live away from his parents in a supervised apartment with the help of staff and friends. His charm and enjoyment of life are contagious. Peter is a full time volunteer at a Food Bank and this spring made a "confession of faith" at his church in Pennsylvania.

Peter has inspired my work at the National Organization on Disability. His handwriting appears on the inside front cover of our most popular publication *That All May Worship*. Thanks to Peter, I have come to believe that it is our responsibility as people of faith to identify and remove barriers to the full participation of children and adults with disabilities in our congregations. As there are no barriers to God's love, there should be no barriers in God's house.

When Your Life Includes A Wheelchair reminds us that wheelchair users face barriers everyday – barriers of architecture as well as barriers of attitude. In her book, Marilyn Willison often addresses these barriers with humor and offers very practical advice to others in similar situations. Woven throughout the book is Marilyn's spirited strength, which has sustained her on her most amazing journey.

I hope you enjoy this book as much as I have. Watch out! This kind of reading can change your life.

Sincerely,

Ginny Thornburgh, Director
Religion and Disability Program
National Organization on Disability
910 Sixteenth Street N.W.
Washington, D.C. 20006
www.nod.org/religion

EDITOR'S COMMENTS

For more that twenty years, Desert Ministries Inc. has persevered in behalf of those in special need. The name of our not-for-profit organization (DMI) refers to the Scripture, especially in Isaiah 35, where it says "The desert will rejoice and blossom when the living water comes." To us the love of God in Christ is the Living Water, which helps all of us endure and survive through the various deserts of our lives; and there are many. The list of some other publications appears at the back of the book.

Here, I am especially proud and pleased to introduce you to another area of challenge. I have been Marilyn Murray Willison's pastor and friend for a long time. I was pleased to officiate at her marriage to Tony: she seated in her wheelchair, he in a Chapel chair beside her. It was great.

Marilyn has a special charm and inspiration in the way she manages her daily life with grace and goodness and dignity. In this volume she shows how gifted she also is as a writer. Her credentials are well proven in her previous publications and current writings. God Bless her! We are proud to have her share this book with us.

• • • • •

We are grateful to Mr. J. D. Thrower, President of Eagle Graphic Services of Ft. Lauderdale, who has devoted exceptional time and creativity and energy in this, as he does in all of our publishing endeavors. He is a committed Christian gentleman and an accomplished professional in his work.

I also thank Mr. Jack Drury, President of the Southeast Region of the Wheelchair Foundation, for his contribution to the publication. Great work is being done by his organization. Please read the information, which appears as an appendix to this publication.

We thank Ginny Thornburgh, from her prestigious position in Washington, for her introduction and affirmative comments. She knows where of she writes.

Our friend Holly Strawbridge once more has provided her excellent professional assistance as copy editor. Thank you.

God bless you all who read this. We will make this book and others available without charge, on your request. Take care. There is a ton of trouble in the world; but more, there are a tremendous lot of people like Marilyn working to overcome it.

Cordially,

Rev. Dr. Richard M. Cromie
President of Desert Ministries, Inc.

 PREFACE

At one time or another, each of us dreams about events in our future life: maybe a yet-to-happen graduation, a wedding or holidays with loved ones. Rarely, however, do we envision a state of declining health. Optimism-oriented professionals would no doubt consider this a good thing. According to the latest figures, one in every five Americans will experience a form of disability at some point in their life. It may be the loss of sight or smell, or the malfunction of a major organ. But the most common and complex form of disability is lack of mobility.

This book is a subjective look at the impact of such a chronic health problem on this writer's life. Back when I was healthy, I never bothered to think about the attitudes and side effects that accompany illness. Perhaps I should have been a bit more spiritual and acquainted myself with Proverbs 16:18 *Pride goes before disaster, and arrogance before a fall.* Back then, I divided people into two categories: those who were healthy, like me, and those who were sick. Because our lifestyles were relatively separated, it took a personal crisis to teach me – to actually force me – to become aware that life exists on many levels.

Years ago, when coping with a ruptured romance, a parenting issue or a personal crisis at the newspaper where I worked, I would quip that "things are so stressful I feel like a raw nerve ending walking through life."

That attempt to rationalize my chaotic lifestyle with humor now seems outrageously ironic. Nowadays, a malfunctioning bundle of raw nerve endings has literally transformed my life, my priorities, and even my personality. Those nerve endings have also transformed the way I remember the circumstances of my once-complicated-but-able-bodied life.

Back when I was young, healthy and felt invincible, I religiously maintained a daily journal into which I entered the events, exchanges and emotions that comprised the tapestry of my ordinary, if turbulent, life. But as my illness assumed increasingly bizarre forms, I became less and less able to rely on my limbs. My right leg grew ominously unsteady, radically curtailing my mobility. My right hand simultaneously became sporadically unreliable, which put an end to playing the piano and writing in my beloved journal. Instead of waiting for a "good day," in which I was able to write steadily, I found that abstinence was easier. So I stopped chronicling my life with a pen and learned to experience it in the heady, emotional and often bewildering stratosphere of "here and now." Because the physical act of writing became so difficult, I substituted rendering my life events, my thoughts and feelings to memory. Essentially, I began to "live" my life rather than "record" it.

Each year millions of Americans lose the ability to walk. For some, like Christopher Reeve, it is the result of an accident. For others, like me, it's because of an illness, in my case Multiple Sclerosis. Either way, there is no denying that losing the use of one's extremities profoundly affects every aspect of life. This little book is designed to help provide a mini roadmap to some of the issues that wheelchair users (and the people who love them) need to know in order to experience a less restrictive and more meaningful life. While my story may not be typical, I welcome the opportunity to share insights, challenges, and discoveries that I wish I had known when I first became wheelchair dependent.

$\approx 1 \backsim$

ILLNESS AND
YOUR RELATIONSHIPS

At the time I became ill, I was health & fitness editor at the Los Angeles Times Syndicate. Oddly enough, I spent my days immersed in reading material about fitness, exercise, nutrition and general body care, and going to lunch or attending meetings with fitness leaders like Bruce Jenner, Nathan Pritikin, and Norman Cousins. Yet I was completely unprepared when faced with the onset of a problem that left me unable to walk properly, much less participate in horseback riding and competitive show jumping (which I did two to three times each week), jogging, dancing, or any other physically rewarding activity.

Not surprisingly, my pre-illness lifestyle was a hectic, high-stress one. I went through a heartbreaking divorce. I had a short-tempered boss who made sure I went home in tears more often than not. And for several months before my walking problems began, my appetite and sleeping patterns were reduced to the bare minimum. In the midst of all the chaos, I juggled two active sons and a wide circle of friends. In retrospect, it's obvious that I spent far too much time burning my candle at both ends. No wonder my health suffered. Stress can and does exacerbate symptoms in a disease like multiple sclerosis.

And thus began a saga that has taught me enough, my friends

joke, to earn my own medical degree. The first neurologist I saw spent 15 minutes testing my reflexes and watching me try to walk steadily before abruptly telling me I had multiple sclerosis and curtly suggesting that I go home and get my affairs in order. After that, I saw an internist who ran a day's worth of tests on me and came to the conclusion that I was an extraordinarily healthy young woman. He said he thought I might have a viral infection, but couldn't confirm that without a spinal tap. I decided that if I were as healthy as he said I was, then my body would surely regain its equilibrium without the added trauma of a spinal puncture and a hospital stay. I was finally learning that, despite a lifetime of robust health, even a self-styled, super-efficient, hyper-productive, adrenalin-propelled Ms. Type A had limits on how much stress a body could bear.

Not too long ago, after years of fighting my physical condition, and hoping, praying and struggling for a "normal life," I realized that regardless of my slow and wobbly penmanship, I had bottled up words that needed to be released. I was no longer able to live with hidden fears and swallowed tears so dangerously close to the surface. Writing three earlier books had taught me that struggling to share my thoughts and feelings with others is the most effective way of clarifying and accepting them for myself. Torturing myself with life's pre- and post-disability differences, I should have been reminded of Ecclesiastes 7:10: *Do not ask why the old days were better than the present; for that is a foolish question.*

As a result, the challenges of my severely restricted life are still present, but they no longer make my life a senseless struggle or an unrewarding existence. As I look back on the process of acknowledging my disability, I see that I have been taught lessons I would otherwise have avoided. I have gained a vantage point from which I can hear and see my life more clearly.

The process of becoming disabled has, blessedly, had its share of positive aspects. I've been forced to slow down and enjoy life, rather than continue on what now, in retrospect, seems like an annoying pursuit of perfection. Lack of mobility has forced me to accept that it is okay to just be me, without accolades or accomplishments. Illness has forced me to enjoy the things I can do and postpone the things I cannot. It has acted like a diluting agent on my perpetual impatience. No longer do I fume if kept waiting or put on hold. Just being part of our remarkable, wonderful world is a gift, so I don't have to insist that life always be orchestrated the way I think it should be played. In some ways, illness has made me calmer, slightly more accepting, hopefully more tolerant and decidedly more appreciative than before.

Illness has also taught me that few things are as psychologically devastating as not having your own mobility. When I hear people complain about trivialities, for example a cold sore or an incorrectly cooked restaurant entrée, I wonder what they would think if they lost their ability to walk. But then I remember that there are many forms of discomfort, and not all of them are as obvious as mine.

My struggle has forced me to see that a strong body is a God-given gift, not merely an unquestioned birthright. This challenging experience has also taught me that ill health can open the door to surprising gifts as well as increased awareness and understanding. Yet I still include in my secret wishes Isaiah's message: *Brace the arms that are limp, steady the knees that give way.*

2

YOUR RELATIONSHIP
WITH YOURSELF

Although a wheelchair user soon learns that established relationships with friends, family, and colleagues irrevocably change, the most important transformation is the relationship you have with yourself when you become disabled. From the vantage point of being in a wheelchair for almost 15 years, it seems there are two choices: acceptance with protest, or acceptance with resignation. Without knowing precisely why, I chose the former.

For most of us, self-image boils down to how we view ourselves under emotional, financial or physical duress. Some people wholeheartedly embrace a challenging lifestyle. And in many ways this makes sense. In today's enlightened world there are endless mechanical, structural, and personal aides to streamline an otherwise compromised lifestyle. This makes it particularly easy to focus and think of yourself as disabled, in the same way a diploma or a certificate changes someone's identity into that of a college graduate, a CPA, or an attorney.

When the arrival of a disability is sudden and severe, the overnight transition to an identity associated with that disability is inescapable. People with spinal cord injuries work long and hard to gain small and slow (very slow) improvements. In situations like mine, the process is an elongated one of very slow and possibly inevitable, decline. The good news is that there is plenty of time to become accustomed to physical losses. The bad news is that it requires strength to accept and adapt without giving up. People struggling with a chronic progressive illness like multiple sclerosis (MS), amyotrophic lateral sclerosis (ALS), or Parkinson's disease learn to adapt gradually and to restructure their self-image incrementally. Those with cerebral palsy or other lifelong conditions that begin in childhood have relatively stable physical challenges.

Re-establishing a healthy relationship with yourself after life has taken a dramatic downturn is no easy task. There are a few things to keep in mind when restructuring your inner life. Perhaps the most helpful realignment is to acknowledge and accept that, after becoming disabled, your identity can no longer rest solely upon what you do. By definition, a disability limits or curtails one's scope of activity, and the resulting loss of "accomplishment" means the ego-driven self-image automatically undergoes a major downshift. But just because you can no longer swim, skydive, play the piano or run a marathon does not mean that you are a less worthy person. It simply means that you are a less physically active person. And that's a huge distinction.

It is important to remember that doing whatever it takes to maintain your self-esteem and positive self-image after a period of illness or diminished health is not only worthwhile, it's essential. A wise friend has reminded me on countless occasions that instead of conducting a continual self-evaluation regarding what I can or cannot do physically, my time would be better spent compiling a mental inventory of character assets. This exercise is a guaranteed mood lifter. Instead of lamenting over the fact that you can't go dancing on a Friday night, why not spend the same block of time doing something that doesn't challenge you physically, like getting together with friends? And if you find yourself edging closer to sorrow and self-pity, do something nice for someone else. A little introspection (as in "What can I do to be of service?") will not only improve your spirits, it will have a positive effect on other people in your life. After all, it's far more important for you to be a thoughtful, non-judgmental, cheerful and pro-actively compassionate person, to exercise your spiritual muscles, than to be buff, blessed with a great backhand, or merely be physically active and athletically fit.

Regardless of your level of disability, try to think of yourself as an emotional or spiritual athlete rather than a physical one. If you keep track of the positive things that you do each day on an inner level, rather than concentrating on your body's achievements, you'll soon discover a growing sense of accomplishment and peace.

Back when this country was much younger, Thoreau reminded Americans that it was important to deal with our inner calm instead of with the hustle and bustle of an externally focused, achievement-oriented lifestyle. In his words, "It's what a man thinks of himself that really determines his fate." One of the best ways to improve your relationship with yourself once your body has limited your physical abilities, is to pay less attention to the achievements and opinions of others.

After a disability, new friendships are often made and old ones fall away simply because sometimes it can be hard to see a "different self" reflected in others' eyes. But if your own vision of yourself is strong and clear, it won't matter quite so much what other people may or may not think about you or how they view your changed circumstances. By the time we are adults, we should be able to make choices based on what we believe is best for us, which takes into account our own physical, spiritual and emotional priorities, rather than living in a state of perpetual anxiety over the opinions of family, friends, colleagues or strangers.

It is without a doubt essential to maintain as good a relationship as possible with yourself after your life circumstances have been drastically altered. As long as you remain confident in your own skin and continue to be your own biggest fan, negative external circumstances will have far less power to upset your emotional equilibrium. And a healthy self-esteem, even if it's trapped in an unhealthy body, is sometimes only a prayer away: 2 Corinthians 4:16 *That is why we never give up. Though our outward humanity is in decay, our inner strength in the Lord is growing every day.*

∾3∾

YOUR RELATIONSHIP WITH GOD

There are a variety of ways to deal with your relationship with God after a traumatic experience. Some people actually become angry with God, feeling that they have been cruelly singled out, or they convince themselves that they are being "punished" for a past transgression. Others think that offering up enough prayers will automatically reverse their body's shortcomings, and believe that the only reason they continue to suffer physically is because not enough prayers have been said. (*Pray without ceasing:* I Thessalonians 5:17) There is a third option, which is the choice to view the challenge as a divinely ordained learning experience. Acceptance, which is not the same as giving up or losing hope, eliminates much of the stress from a bad physical situation.

Many years ago, a friend sent me a beautiful poem regarding the wisdom of looking at life like a finely stitched tapestry. The message is that while God sees the finished product on one side (imagine the two sides of an intricate oriental rug), we see only the twisted, tangled and confusing underside. It's hard to make sense of such chaos. The poem's message is that just because we aren't able to see God's grand plan for our lifespan doesn't mean that an overall design comprised of beauty, logic, and achievement doesn't exist.

Whatever your religious beliefs before your disability, the connection you feel with God will have a profound effect on how well you cope with this new and different stage of your life.

People who don't believe in God, or who are uncomfortable calling on a higher power for help, may find their already difficult situation becomes worse. Proverbs 3:5 *"Put all your trust in the Lord and do not rely on your own understanding."* When your life is turned upside down, it is not a weakness to acknowledge fear or sorrow, or to ask for help and support. Continually pretending that everything in your life is just fine is denial. No matter how great things are, sooner or later you are going to encounter frustrations, disappointments and hurts that will call for some much needed, but possibly rusty, spiritual coping skills.

Please do not feel that God is ignoring your prayers just because your physical condition does not improve. Those prayers may be bringing you blessings that have more to do with what you need than with what you want. I have learned that even if your legs don't work, your life can develop new and incredibly rewarding facets that – had you enjoyed perfect health – might not have come your way.

If you've asked yourself why God could let illness or disability take over your life, it might help to remember that God never promised that life would be fair. What He did promise is that no matter what challenges we might face, His help is ours for the asking. Belief in divine help is one factor that makes difficulties bearable. And that just might explain why Psalm 23 has been such a source of comfort for so many years: *The Lord is my shepherd: therefore can I lack nothing. He shall feed me in a green pasture: and lead me forth beside the waters of comfort. He shall con-*

vert my soul: and bring me forth in the paths of righteousness, for his Name's sake. Yea, though I walk through the valley of the shadow of death, I will fear no evil: for thou art with me; thy rod and thy staff comfort me. Thou shalt prepare a table before me against them that trouble me: thou hast anointed my head with oil, and my cup shall be full. But thy loving-kindness and mercy shall follow me all the days of my life: and I will dwell in the house of the Lord for ever.

YOUR RELATIONSHIP
WITH YOUR SPOUSE OR PARTNER

There are four essential ingredients for maintaining a success-ful relationship with your spouse or partner when you have a life altering -- particularly a mobility-challenging -- disability. These are strength, empathy, compassion, and a healthy sense of humor.

Strength becomes an issue for both of you on a physical and an emotional level. When your body refuses to cooperate, a vast number of ordinary and/or tedious chores become the other per-son's problem. This includes not only general everyday activities like cooking, cleaning, and grooming, but also the additional challenge of helping get your body from Point A to Point B. Nasty little surprises like muscle spasms, cramps, loss of balance or falls, means that one person becomes a physical caretaker while the other becomes the (sometimes reluctant) recipient of a loved one's concern or sorrow or frustration. As long as the bonds of love and respect are strong enough, those unpleasant physical intimacies can generate heartfelt gratitude and a deeper connection.

Empathy is essential because it can sometimes be a challenge for someone in good health to anticipate or understand the needs of a person whose body is in a constant, often painful, state of revolt. Having a partner who possesses an empathetic character is like the blessing that describes the virtuous women in Proverbs 31:10 *For her price is far above rubies.*

Compassion is required because it defuses the inevitable and unpleasant eruptions of irritability or impatience. Few people who enjoy excellent health can understand the challenges of a body that routinely disobeys or ignores its owner's commands. But a compassionate heart is able to relate, understand, and even share the physical and emotional challenges that accompany such a disability.

Sense of Humor. Probably the most important (and sometimes hardest to achieve) ingredient for a sustained, loving relationship is a good, shared sense of humor. While it might be basic human nature to regard physical problems with a sense of drama, despair or anxiety, the fact remains that any number of situations are, quite simply, funny. If you live with someone wise enough to accept your body's bizarre behavior as a source of humor, you are blessed indeed. And if you can accept recalcitrant nerves, muscles and mobility aids as occasional sources of unexpected "situational entertainment," you'll be better off, as well.

When I first became a wheelchair user, one of the difficulties I wrestled with was the fear that I would spend the rest of my life alone. Any woman who is on her own due to choice, divorce, or because she has not yet found Mr. Right, can't help but wonder whether or not her life would be enhanced by having a special someone with whom to share life's moments. Because I'm a hopeless romantic, that was an issue that weighed heavily on me when I lost my ability to walk, and it made my disability an especially bitter pill to swallow.

Even though I had been a divorced mom for many years, being single and (obviously) disabled introduced a whole new

14

unwelcome level of loneliness. Within weeks of becoming wheelchair dependent, I couldn't help but notice a dramatic difference in how my appeal – real or imagined – seemed to have instantly evaporated. In the twinkling of an eye, I realized that men no longer flirted, smiled, or went out of their way to spend time with me. Feeling that my potential for romance had evaporated along with my mobility turned out to be particularly challenging.

So, imagine my surprise, when I found someone who loved me regardless of my physical disabilities seven years after I lost my ability to walk. It is important to know that such improbable happenings do occur. Just as my mother told me, when you stop looking, it happens.

Perhaps because my husband fell in love with me after I became disabled, our relationship has not been sabotaged by a "surprise" illness. If your partner or spouse expected to be with you in health rather than in sickness, your relationship needs to be prepared for some challenging episodes. I know of two marriages that collapsed under the weight of an unexpected disability. The missing element in those relationships was the ability of one partner to bear the undeniably heavy weight of caring for and caring about a loved one in the face of severe physical challenges. There's no mention of how paralysis can threaten a marriage in Corinthians, but when I (in my wheelchair) joyously married a remarkable (able-bodied) man who loved me, we chose this passage to share with our wedding guests: *"Love is patient, love is kind, and is not jealous; love does not brag and is not arrogant, does not act unbecomingly; it does not seek its own, is not provoked, does not take into account a wrong suffered."*

It might help to remember Dana Reeve's words to her husband, Christopher, after his paralyzing accident. When he realized the extent of his injuries and questioned the value of continuing life, she begged him to not give up hope and reminded him that his family needed him, that she loved him, and that mobile or not, he was still the person she fell in love with. That basic message is important for all of us to remember when we face life's challenges; we can only hope and pray that the people who love us, love who we are more than they love what we are able to do.

5

YOUR RELATIONSHIP
WITH YOUR CHILDREN

Perhaps the most poignant aspect of my disability adjustment was the shift that occurred in my relationship with my
sons. Although we are extraordinarily close now, I deeply regret
the lost time and missed experiences that my illness imposed on
my relationship with them when they were teenagers. No longer
was I "Super-Mom," who baked homemade cookies every
Monday, competed in horse shows on weekends, took piano lessons, hosted periodic dinner parties, and worked as a full-time
journalist. Instead, I became a shadow of my formerly high-
speed self. Worse, I became someone my children had to adapt
to and worry about.

Perhaps because I've always taken motherhood very seriously, it was particularly painful when my malfunctioning muscles
forced me out of important parts of my sons' lives. Because of
my immobility, I missed family activities, proms, parties, shopping expeditions, school visits, and sporting events that, had I
been physically healthy, I would have taken for granted.

Conventional wisdom tells us that children are resilient, and
it is true. But resiliency doesn't override the fact that great challenges still affect young people. It is important to remember that
change is not necessarily an entirely negative thing. In some ways

illness and disability can have beneficial effects on the young people whose lives are touched by an unanticipated challenge.

If you are concerned about the new realities of your family situation, it helps to remember that what is lost in physical terms can be more than made up for in emotional growth. Don't underestimate a child's capacity to adapt and exhibit a youthful wisdom about your body's new limitations.

Instead of feeling guilty and sad because illness has interfered with your original parenting plan, why not tally the unexpected strengths your child will likely gain from seeing a much-loved adult cope with a major life challenge? No youngster wishes to have a physically impaired parent, but having one can more effectively build character and teach a young person coping skills and a charitable frame of mind than a lifetime of parental lectures.

YOUR RELATIONSHIP
WITH THE WORLD AT LARGE

After I came to terms with my own limited mobility, what amazed me was not so much how a wheelchair changed my view of life, but how much the wheelchair changed the way I was viewed by others. All too often, able-bodied people have trouble separating ability from mobility, and personal power from physical strength. They see the chair, and then they see me.

Actors Christopher Reeve and Daryl Mitchell (of Veronica's Closet) and Singer Teddy Pendergrass are three good-looking celebrities who also learned this the hard way. My own wheelchair-restricted existence has taught me that, in today's world, appearance is far more important than I ever realized. Those whose bodies are altered by accident or illness often find their lives transformed in ways that transcend the physical. The frustration of adapting to changes in independence, accessibility and income reverberate long after mere "body issues" have been resolved.

Although I lost my ability to walk, it didn't take long to accept that high heels, running shoes and riding boots would no longer be a part of my life. It was, however, much harder to accept the transition from being perceived as a competent, pleasant looking professional to merely being a woman in a wheelchair.

When my metal and vinyl wheelchair comes into view, people don't notice my manicure or makeup, and they rarely take the chance to discover what my personality might be like, because they bring their own prejudice and discomfort to our encounter. *"The poor, sick dear, and oh, she has such a pretty face, too."*

I always get a chuckle when I tell people that I used to be 5' 6" tall, but now I'm 3' 3"! Despite how others see me, I am the same person as before. The only change is that my legs simply don't work these days.

Loss of mobility abruptly expels an otherwise attractive person from mainstream life. The truth is that sooner or later, we're all going to have to change the way we see ourselves. Time will ensure that. Illness hastens self-image adjustment, but no one escapes the changes of aging. There is no doubt that physical beauty is powerful, but it does not last forever, no matter who you are.

It is embarrassing to admit what an initial struggle it was for me to deal with the vanity side of paraplegia. I silently railed against being overlooked or devalued simply because I could no longer walk. It was a tearful time. *And God shall wipe away all tears from their eyes; and there shall be no more death, neither sorrow, nor crying, neither shall there be any more pain: for the former things are passed away.* Revelations 21:4

Today, thousands of days later, I have stopped thinking of life before and after paraplegia as "better" or "worse." I no longer divide the chapters of my life into categories labeled "good" and "bad." I am finally able to treasure what was and cherish what is, and I try to remember to do so with a non-disabled, sincere smile.

I've learned that while my body is forced to do less, my mind seems desperate to do more. Some of what it does is wonderful:

I write, read and think with renewed discipline. But emotionally, I am still susceptible to frustration beyond anything I ever imagined. When I drop something I can't pick up, or feel let down by someone I was counting on, or I wish I were free to join in others' fun, the sense of gloom and doom can be overwhelming. On the other hand, I've learned to say "please" and "thank you" and "I'm sorry" with a frequency and fluency that would surely be a bit less automatic to an able-bodied person.

When I searched for scriptures that mention the word smile, I came up empty handed. The closest I could find is in Proverbs 17:22 *"A glad heart makes for good health."* What I think this means is that if you can take the time and effort to put a smile on your face, regardless of how fearful or discouraged you might feel on the inside, you'll be surprised at both the obvious and invisible benefits it pays for yourself and others.

When I first became a wheelchair user, I was bothered – sometimes downright irritated – by people who failed to make eye contact with me, or by their body language, make it clear that they were avoiding me. It didn't take me too long to see that they were probably responding to and reflecting back my own level of discomfort with disability. It only took one small experiment in which I smiled at everyone to convince me that so long as I looked comfortable and pleasant, even strangers would respond with warmth and kindness.

Unfortunately, there are still lots of people in this world who are so caught up in their own lives and issues that it doesn't occur to them to lend a hand or share a cheerful sentiment. But by and large, I have found that if I initiate a pleasant encounter, with a smile or a small, silent prayer, others follow my lead.

My husband has long believed that the majority of negative behavior patterns stem from repressed, unacknowledged, or misdirected fear. When he hears that someone has behaved unkindly or in anger, his first question is "I wonder what he (or she) is afraid of?" Once I realized that most able-bodied people have some level of fear regarding their own health or mobility or independence, it made it a lot easier for me to counteract their unconscious fear level with a silent prayer of peace and contentment. Remember, people are often afraid that the disabled might ask them for help, which could put them in the uncomfortable position of being unable to do whatever is needed.

Years ago, I heard a quote about how it actually takes fewer muscles to smile than to frown. Whether or not it's true, the reality is that for those of us with physical challenges, a pleasant manner and smiling face will generally counteract the countless obstacles of every disabled day.

Some remarkable research about coping with adversity has shown that attitude is the most important element when it comes to effectively managing a chronic illness. Dr. Paul Pearsall studied people who live with chronic illness and classified two distinct categories: those who survive and those who thrive. According to his book, The Beethoven Factor, being cheerful pays huge dividends. "Surviving is coping; thriving is creating. . . . Master thrivers, who aren't likely to see the end of their suffering yet still manage to savor life . . . showed three distinct skills: they were able to laugh in the face of their adversity, to argue effectively against their own negative self-defeating thoughts, and to find something positive about their situation." Why not give it a try?

YOUR RELATIONSHIP WITH MONEY

Isaiah 55:1 *Come and drink – even if you have no money. Come, take your choice of wine and milk – it's all free.*

The financial lessons of a chronic neurological disorder like mine are legion. Because I had no health insurance, every physical therapy session, every exam, every treatment was costly with a capital C. While my medical expenses have not yet reached a million dollars, I have spent enough to buy a few middle-class suburban homes. Within one decade, I wiped out every cent I had saved. As a result, like millions of Americans in today's troubled economy, I no longer have financial security. And as anyone who has ever been seriously ill knows, when the body doesn't function properly, it's very difficult to earn a living. For a journalist like me, who carried her passport in her purse in case an editor might assign a spur-of-the-moment foreign deadline, being housebound brought my career to a screeching halt just when medical expenses were soaring.

Unless you are independently wealthy or are lucky enough to have rich and generous loved ones, disability will dramatically affect your financial well-being. Most people think that a mobility disability means life is changed primarily because of dependence on a wheelchair. But, in reality, every aspect of your physical, emotional, social, and financial life changes. Fifty million Americans have a serious disability, and 70% of us are unemployed, which means the disabled are economically disadvantaged.

When you add the high-cost expense of equipment and assistance to an already reduced income, something's got to give. The last time I had to buy a new wheelchair (they cost about $1,000 and last approximately six or seven years), I tried to rationalize the painful expense by thinking of how much I would have spent during the same time period if I'd been walking and had worn out shoes that needed to be replaced.

If you need to downsize your lifestyle because your body's demands have stretched your finances to the limit, there's no shame in investigating new or alternative spending patterns. Since I've been in a wheelchair, I've tried to initiate a new approach to my budgetary constraints. At first I worried relentlessly about a reduced lifestyle. But it didn't take long for me to realize that there was no benefit in whining. That's when I became the Queen of the Bargain Hunters. I'm willing to bet that if you turn penny pinching and bargain hunting into an enjoyable quest, you'll manage to save money and have fun doing it. If anyone had told me 20 years ago that I would approach saving money as a game, I never would have believed it. But rearranging your spending habits is just one more way that a disability can be approached as a learning process rather than a lifestyle catastrophe.

8

LESSONS I HAVE LEARNED

I often think of my enforced wheelchair sentence as nothing more than a rather bizarre and character-building learning experience. To that end, I've compiled a haphazard collection of things I have learned during my years as a paraplegic, things I wish I had not had to learn the hard way:

1. ORGANIZE YOUR LIFE. As long as it's hard to get to places and reach things you need, it helps to make sure that you know where things have been placed. At one time I was relatively haphazard about my possessions, but these days I know precisely where everything is located in my house, from a spool of chartreuse thread to the Christmas tree stand. If you take the time to know the whereabouts of everything you have, you'll eliminate frustration from your own life and from the lives of people who need to know where the Phillips screwdriver or the masking tape might be.

2. KNOW YOUR BATHROOMS. Among the unfortunate side effects of immobility are the many complications that arise surrounding use of the bathroom. I have learned to tailor my activities around the availability of a good-sized restroom with handrails. The good news is that every McDonald's has a handicapped bathroom that is actually functional for people

whose legs don't work. The bad news is that no matter how well you plan, there will be times when you and your bodily functions will be at a decided disadvantage. Reynolds Price wrote honestly and touchingly about such problems in his remarkable book A Whole New Life. "Even now after the passage of the well-meaning but so far toothless act for disabled Americans, . . . bathrooms have been designed by some vaguely well-intentioned but able-bodied planner with no clear sense of what's required by an actual human with paralyzed or even weakened limbs . . . As a brief introduction to the [bathroom] problems of the lame, if you're an able-bodied man or woman in trousers, attempt the chore. Sit parallel to a standard toilet, fully dressed, in a narrow chair. Deny yourself the power to rise by even an inch. Now, work your pants and underwear to below your knees. Now, using only your hands and arms – *do not cheat with your legs; they're mere dead wood;* don't try to press your weight on your feet – slide or hop somehow from your chair to the toilet, complete your business without mishap, reverse the motion and redress yourself. All but impossible, if you're not a professional acrobat."

3. LEARN TO ASK FOR WHAT YOU NEED. One of the side effects of life in a wheelchair is that people often tend to assume that they know what you want or what you need. Rarely will they ask for your input. For that reason, I speak up and let people know if I need help and tell them exactly what I need. There was a time when I was reluctant to draw attention to my recalcitrant limbs by asking for help, but time has taught me to swallow my pride and explain when I need help opening a door, reaching for something, or even a compassionate shoulder to cry on. *Ask, and it shall be given you; seek, and ye shall find; knock, and it shall be opened unto you.*

4. LEARN TO TAILOR YOUR APPETITE TO YOUR ACTIVITY.

This is probably not a newsflash to able-bodied people, but those of us in wheelchairs tend to gain more weight than we would like. When you can't exercise on a regular basis and normal daily movement is restricted, the metabolism slows and the waistline grows. The only way I've managed to keep from gaining loads and loads of unwanted weight is to completely rethink the topic of food. If I were to continue to eat the three square daily meals that I once consumed, heaven only knows how much heavier I would be. And when you can't move with ease – or when you must rely on others for help – every extra pound is a disadvantage. I'm not sure about the rules of physics or leverage when it comes to pushing your own body weight in a wheelchair, but I do know that it's a constant struggle to sacrifice tempting calories day after day to retain the mobility I still have.

5. TRY NOT TO BE IRRITATED BY INSENSITIVITY. I like to think that when I was able bodied, I was thoughtful and patient with disabled people. The truth is that I never even thought about what other people's lives might be like, because I was obsessed with my own concerns. I try to remember my own years of able-bodied tunnel-vision inattentiveness when absent-minded shoppers let a store door close in front of my wheelchair or when other incidents make my life more difficult. I think it's important to remember that no one can really be expected to understand the difficulties you face when all they've known is good health. As far as I'm concerned, it just makes the rare and wonderful people who can mentally put themselves in your place that much more valuable. When you are on the verge of snapping or sulking, it helps to remember William James' observation that "The art of being wise is the art of knowing what to overlook."

6. REDESIGN YOUR WARDROBE. When you are unable to stand, putting on and taking off clothes is a genuine challenge. For a former chotheshorse like me, becoming a wheelchair wardrobe victim was particularly painful. Shopping, once considered the ultimate fun experience, turned into an unpalatable chore. Luckily, I have discovered some nice boutiques that allow me to take items home, try them on in privacy, and bring them back if they don't fit. Dressing rooms are simply not designed to accommodate people with special mobility needs. When it comes to clothes, the crucial factor is no longer fabric, color or style; it's how easy it is to put on and take off. A few years ago, I turned up my nose at the thought of elasticized waistbands. I learned the hard way, however, that no matter how attractive an outfit looks, if it's a struggle to get on and off, it simply isn't worth the bother. All my shorts and trousers have zippers and elastic, and it still takes me thirty minutes or more to get dressed each day. I recently read about a wheelchair-bound former actress who has created a whole new career for herself by designing attractive clothes for those of us who have trouble getting dressed. Hooray for her!

7. PREPARE TO ECONOMIZE. When you were able-bodied you may have enjoyed shopping at certain stores, dining in your favorite restaurants, and generally enjoying a familiar lifestyle. Unless you are very lucky, however, or win the lottery, you will probably have to reduce your spending once you can no longer walk.

8. LOOK FOR THE LESSONS IN THIS EXPERIENCE. Dr. Bernie Siegel, author of best selling _Love, Medicine & Miracles_ firmly believes that a health crisis can be a form of renewal. If we spend too much time focusing on the past, we may never be able to find the benefits that accompany a medical

problem. Your benefit may be increased sensitivity, a renewed relationship with family members, a deeper appreciation of life's little pleasures, or a more patient outlook on life. Whatever it is, I promise that you will learn something about yourself, about the people with whom you share your heart or about life in general thanks to what has happened to your body.

9. CHERISH THE INDEPENDENCE YOU HAVE. I think it is important to not rely on others more than is absolutely necessary. You will find an entirely new wellspring of pleasure when it comes to things like privacy, financial autonomy, and a sense of accomplishment, when you surrender the smallest possible portion of your independence. People who love you can be expected to question your ability to cope on your own. But I firmly believe that you will be far happier in the long run if you force yourself to adapt to your new circumstances rather than crying out for help every time you face a difficulty. Alone in my kitchen recently, I dropped a mug, and slowly managed to clean the spilled coffee from the floor all by myself. What would have taken someone else five minutes took me close to one hour, but when the task was finished, I felt flushed with victory and radiant the rest of the day!

10. KNOW THAT EVERYONE HAS SOME FORM OF DISABILITY. I used to feel that being singled out to suffer paralyzed legs was some sort of sick cosmic joke. Time has taught me, however, that being in a wheelchair is not the worst of all possible fates. Some people have perfectly functioning bodies, but are tormented by mental or emotional difficulties. And some people have physical disabilities that are not readily visible. Once you realize that you can handle the cross you bear, it will help you accept that things could always be worse. When I'm in the throes of a pity party, I remind myself how grim my life would be if I

-- the ultimate media junkie -- had lost my vision instead of my mobility. This train of thought leads to the next step, which is being thankful that my situation, however challenging, is not without its blessings.

9

MORE LESSONS I HAVE LEARNED

After watching me work on this manuscript for months, Tony asked to read what I'd written so far. After he turned the last page, he looked up and told me it was very good. Then he paused, cleared his throat, and said, "I think, however, you may have forgotten one very important aspect. You have told people how your life has changed, and you've mentioned several of the things you had to give up, but you've failed to tell them about the proactive things you've done to restructure your life since you became disabled."

Taken aback by my husband's remarkable insight, I gave his observation some thought and realized that he was absolutely right. Contrary to conventional wisdom, people whose bodies change and abilities decline are more often than not surprisingly pleasant people. How can that be? In my observations, it's because we are all magnificent creatures who inherently – even instinctively -- strive to make the best of bad situations. Bearing that in mind, here are a few thoughts about how I've reconfigured my life. Consider these as general guidelines or individual suggestions, because what works for one person may be inappropriate for someone else.

1. FIND WAYS TO SOCIALIZE AND CELEBRATE.
When I moved back to the USA from Great Britain, I quickly learned that my compact Florida home was located on a street full of cheerful neighbors who regularly dropped in for a visit or to ask if I needed anything. Our street is a highly Americanized mini United Nations. I moved here from London, Maurizio next door hails from Milan, Inga, two houses away, is from Norway, Reina, farther up the street, is from Holland, Samantha is from Canada, the Arvezus and the Acosta families are from Cuba, Harold is from Sweden, Tomas and Max are from Germany, Gudrun is from Austria, and Anu is from India. I'm telling you about my neighborhood because it explains why my latest "party girl" incarnation is my favorite. Because my house is the only one on the street with a ramp instead of steps to the front door, I have not been able to visit many of my neighbors. This type of "barrier" is the type of thing that made me worry that my social life would be restricted or non-existent.

Then I remembered a passage I'd read in the Delany Sisters' book Having Our Say. Sadie was recalling a problem she had experienced in New York in 1920. As she wrestled with her dilemma she realized "You had to decide – am I going to change the world, or am I going to change me Or maybe change the world a little bit, just by changing me?"

So I decided to compensate my immobility by inviting everyone to bring something tasty to my house for neighborhood potluck parties. I provide the drinks and the house and, since cooking is no longer part of my lifestyle, everyone else brings interesting things to eat. Although I do little more than sit and smile, my neighbors think I'm a real Pearl Mesta. I've thrown open my doors this way three or four times a year since moving in, but recent Christmas parties have become some of the happiest events of my life. Our to-the-ceiling tree is laden with a lifetime of treasured ornaments. Friends and neighbors catch up on the news and converse in like countless foreign languages. Dave, my friend Colleen's husband, plays show tunes, Christmas Carols and rock and roll on the baby grand piano. And although I can't join the couples who dance to "Crocodile Rock," my friend Cathy and I have made it an annual tradition to cluster by the keyboard to sing a spirited, if slightly off-key, duet of "Desperado."

There have been times when I've had flashbacks to parties I had given in the past. These days I don't walk my guests to and from my front door, I don't wear an evening gown, and I don't accept compliments on my culinary skills with a benign smile. I am no longer able to stand on my own two feet, assume that money will always be there whenever I need it, or rest assured that life will simply continue to get better and better. But I can rely on the fact that, despite weak legs, an anemic bank account, and my lack of independence, I will always have friends who are ready, willing and able to share in whatever it is I choose to celebrate. That knowledge is a treasure that this party girl will hoard in her heart forever and ever.

2. THERE'S MORE THAN ONE WAY TO KEEP IN TOUCH. Another unpleasant side effects of my physical condition is that my right arm and hand simply refuse to cooperate. Although I've taught myself to needlepoint and occasionally scribble an important phone number or message with my left hand, writing and typing are activities that no longer play a functional role in my life. For a writer, this has been an unsettling and unpleasant development. The part of me that is hopelessly old-fashioned and romantic still prefers nice stationery, pretty greeting cards, and handwritten thank you notes. But, since it

takes me an inordinate amount of time to laboriously address an envelope or scribble a gift card, I've learned to embrace shortcuts wherever possible.

Several years ago my stepdaughter, Laura, graciously gave me an imminently practical birthday gift of pre-addressed, self-adhesive mailing labels. This made it easy for me to send cards and clippings to the important people in my life. There was a time when I would send long, chatty typewritten letters to loved ones who lived far away, but that, too, is now beyond my digital ability. Instead, I let people know they're in my thoughts by keeping pre-addressed 6" x 9" manila envelopes within easy reach to be filled with newspaper or magazine articles that cross my path and might be of interest to them. People I love in London, Amsterdam, Cape Cod and California never know when they'll receive a bulging envelope full of newspaper and magazine cartoons and/or articles that have brought them to mind. The people who populate my address book like to know that I think of them fondly on occasions other than standard Hallmark holidays. My friends tell me they love seeing one of my envelopes arrive in the mail, especially on a day when an envelope is as good as a hug.

If you're not a compulsive newspaper and magazine reader like I am, don't forget the value of the telephone or email. When I first became disabled, I spent several months in mental hibernation and isolation. My emotions were such a tangled mess that I didn't answer letters, phone calls, or extended offers of help; and I now regret it. Over the years I've learned the value of keeping in touch with old friends and doing whatever it takes to make new ones. I may not be able to send handwritten notes or drive a car, but I can still stay connected to the people I treasure with the help on an envelope and a few stamps.

3. TAILOR YOUR TRANSPORTATION. In my past, I owned a variety of European cars, including a bright red Austin Healey, an uber-practical Volvo, and three different Jaguar sedans. These days, however, practicality trumps looks when it comes to getting my wheelchair and me from point A to point B. Now I have a Dodge van with an automatic wheelchair ramp and security straps that transport me safely wherever my whims – and my helper -- take me.

4. THE GIFT OF GIVING. Since I've been in a wheelchair, I've learned a whole new way to shop for and give gifts. Once upon a time, I would buy gifts while on "mission specific shopping trips." I would spend lengthy amounts of time shopping until the perfect gift item jumped out at me. These days, I adapt to my limitations by using an "advance planning" strategy that allows my helper and me to choose, wrap, and mail gifts from an inventory of at-home goodies. Because going out can be a production that involves variables like low energy levels, uncooperative limbs, inhospitable shopping venues, inclement weather, when I do go shopping, I bring home items that will be given to just the right person as much as six months later. And because shopping at Christmastime can be extra challenging, I start composing my gift list as soon as Easter is over. My helper and I spend hot summer days assembling and wrapping custom-made baskets tailor-made for friends and loved ones. They remain stored under my husband's piano until Thanksgiving, when they make their way to the post office. Advance planning, list making, and (in a pinch) catalog shopping lets me play as big a role in holidays as any able-bodied person I know.

5. GIVING HEIRLOOMS FROM THE HEART. No longer being able to live a fast-paced lifestyle really has had its share of unexpected blessings. One of the nicest surprise benefits

is that I have lots of spare time to satisfy my passion for needle-point. Instead of racing around as a journalist in a newspaper office, riding at the stables, or making a fool of myself at a skating rink, spending my waking hours in a recliner chair has made it possible for me to make a variety of special, often personalized gifts for friends and loved ones, one left-handed stitch at a time. When I feel myself slipping into the quicksand of paraplegia-powered low self-esteem, I pull out a small-sized photo album I keep full of snapshots of pillows, belts, ornamental chair sets, and rugs I have made for myself and others. It doesn't have to be needlework. Customized photo albums, scrapbooks, or any creation made by hand and from the heart is guaranteed to enhance your life, not to mention your relationships.

6. LEARN THE THRILL OF THE HUNT. I like to think that MS has really honed my ability for skillful substitution. For everything I have lost, I've tried to find a workable replacement. If you can approach your own disability this way, I am willing to bet that you'll create a different, rather than a diminished, life. One of my favorite substitutions is bargain hunting. When recent transportation problems kept me homebound for more than a month, I realized that my spirits had been sinking. I was suffering from a classic case of cabin fever. It finally dawned on me that the culprit was my favored bargain hunting expeditions, which I had unconsciously used to replace the sense of competence or achievement that I previously got from physical activities. I no longer bring home horse show ribbons or see my byline in a newspaper every week, but I do have other trophies. While an antique store discovery or a bargain first edition may not be the type of achievement I once thoughtlessly took for granted, there are a million different ways to give yourself high-five moments. You just have to find the ones that work for you, your

interests and your level of disability.

7. LOW-MAINTENANCE. My husband would never let me get away with describing my customized lifestyle without including the issue of vanity. For most of my life I've had a certain look, documented in dozens of photo albums in our bookcase. I had ponytail-length hair, oodles of high-heeled shoes, long glossy fingernails, and a serious working woman's wardrobe. But it didn't take a whole lot of time for me to figure out that my psyche could no longer afford to cling to a look that, for better or worse, simply didn't work for me any more.

Years ago I wrote an article for Allure Magazine about vanity versus the wheelchair and, as a result, decided to tailor my appearance to my life instead of vice versa. Taking care of long hair when it's hard to hold a comb is a challenge I can do without. Ditto for little buttons, pantyhose, and anything that is difficult to put on and take off. First the heels and the silk dresses were dispatched to charities, then my fingernails and finally my pony-tailed hair were drastically shortened. Guess what? It's very liberating to go from a stressed-out to a stress-free appearance. If you are wrestling with an impaired or uncooperative body, then this is the time to pick and choose a wardrobe and a personal style that works with your limitations. There are a million different ways to look good. If it helps, just tell yourself that you've "updated" your style. It will be the truth!

8. THINK OF YOURSELF AS AN AMBASSADOR. Private schools seem to be the norm these days, but when I was a student in the 1960's, it was a different world. Back then, going to school in a uniform was definitely out of the ordinary, and our teachers never missed an opportunity to remind us that wherever we went and whatever we did, our uniforms advertised that we represented our school.

In a strange way, the same is true for those of us with disabilities. You may be the only disabled person the man behind the counter at Starbucks, the letter carrier, or the meter maid comes in contact with. If they encounter someone who is sloppy, grumpy, or demanding, guess what assumptions they'll make about the rest of us who are physically challenged? Flip that scenario over, and think what a positive impression it makes when you extend the effort to look and act as pleasantly as possible.

Last year at a theater performance, a very pretty young woman led Tony and me to our seats. When we arrived, she handed us programs, smiled at me, and said, "It's so nice – and unusual – to see a happy person in a wheelchair. Thank you for smiling!" That brief encounter reminded me that, unfortunately for the world at large, people with health problems tend to be seen as real downers. Let's go against the grain on this one.

~10~

EVERYDAY ISSUES

A compromised body comes with its share of emotional booby traps. Being aware of these potential problems can help you avoid unwelcome surprises:

1. FRUSTRATION. To be honest, I don't really enjoy the task of reexamining the "altered lifestyle" my illness imposed on me. What has kept me sane, I'm sure, is my tendency to ignore or overlook the limitations that hostile nerves and muscles have brought my way. Of course, no matter how hard I try, I can't ignore the sense of dependency or the limited mobility that accompanies life in a wheelchair. And I still haven't found a way to overlook how difficult it is to deal with the frustration I experience countless times each week when I have to re-categorize what was once a given (like getting bathed or showered and dressed each morning) into a "help needed" maneuver. Once-simple tasks now require advance planning, the assistance of another human being, and lots of patience, my least favorite word. How sad that spontaneity becomes the first casualty in the minefield lives of the mobility challenged.

One quality-of-life lesson that disability has taught me is that little things are often far more distressing than major ones. For example, I was able to pack away my tailored riding gear and donate my evening gowns and high heels to charity without so much as a sniffle. But I have shed torrents of frustrated tears over dropped or spilled items of little or no value. Go figure!

For the purposes of analysis, there are four realms with which I have wrestled frustration for the past several years: physical, emotional, financial, and social. When it comes to my body, MS has taught me first and foremost how to lovingly lower my expectations. I am no longer able to issue mental commands, such as "bend down," "reach up," or "roll over." with any assurance that arms, legs, hands, and fingers will obey. The physical benefits of years of dancing, jogging, typing, horseback riding, and practicing the piano have evaporated. Based on my abilities today, it's as if I had always led a sedentary lifestyle.

Once I thought that learning a variety of skills would pay great dividends. I now know that the future is often full of unplanned insights. So, instead of working on my fouettes, I've learned how to call for help when I've fallen from my wheelchair. Instead of mastering the finger placement for a Chopin nocturne, I've learned to write and needlepoint with my left instead of my right. There are sandals and easy pull-on and pull-off clothes instead of high heels and terribly chic little black dinner dresses. And there are assisted baths and shampoos, where once there were stand-up showers and lengthy luxurious bubble baths. My hands are too unreliable to take chances with makeup or mascara. So the me you see today is an unenhanced, basic, deeply dependent version of the person I used to be.

2. LONELINESS. In Susan Jeffers' excellent book _Feel The Fear And Do It Anyway_, she writes about a job applicant named Charles whom she met during her work with The Floating Hospital in New York. Charles had a profound impact on the

entire staff. He had been a tough ghetto gang member until he was paralyzed from the waist down by a gunshot wound during a street fight. The author recounts a day she saw Charles, reformed and being retrained as a teacher, talking with a group of youngsters. The children were full of curiosity about what it was like for him to live in a wheelchair. That's when Charles asked them what they thought a handicapped person would want more than anything in the world. Money? Better housing? More or better rehabilitation? His honest, poignant answer was **"friends."**

When I read about Charlie's conversation with his students, I couldn't help but be moved. Like so many once-active people, I too have learned to place a high premium on the people who really know what it means to be a friend.

Lack of mobility, alas, has forced me to partially redefine friendship. And even though I balk at the admission, I have spent lots and lots of time with people I really don't even know; people who, nevertheless, have amused, entertained, and informed me; people who have seen to it that I feel far less isolated than I otherwise might. They are the people who come to me through the television set whenever I need their company. And since I have been in a wheelchair, I have grown to regard these electronic personalities as my friends.

Now that so many of my days and nights are spent at home, I have an added reason to be glad that my father taught me to think of the television as a tool. People who lead lives that are relatively constricted tend to develop a chronic codependency with their television sets. And even though I am blessed with remarkably caring friends and neighbors, the bitter truth is that, because they have busy and demanding lives of their own, I often spend more hours each day with my televised "pals" than with the flesh and blood ones.

3. DEPENDENCE. Perhaps the most painful lesson I have learned in a wheelchair is that illness and isolation often appear as unwelcome Siamese twins. For an extrovert like me, it came as a rude surprise to discover that mobility is an uncontested requirement for membership in mainstream life. Although more and more stores, restaurants and theaters are handicap accessible, getting from point A to point B still requires assistance. The third hand that I often need to get through a doorway, use an ATM, or to gain access to a public restroom, is there only if some kind individual is ready, willing and able to volunteer time. And friends – even the very best – have full lives and countless obligations of their own. The time when you most wish you were not alone is guaranteed to be the time when you will be.

Like a divorcee who finds herself no longer welcome in a couples world, the person who is ill will all too soon discover that he/she lives in a totally different universe from healthy peers unless an effort is made to create a new social life.

4. FEAR. Decades ago, Dr. Normal Vincent Peale taught millions of Americans that positive thinking could help affect the outcome of practically any problem. If you allow yourself to be afraid it's almost like slamming a spiritual door in the face of God.

Years ago I was told that freedom from fear was as simple as access to the airwaves. But although television and radio programs are always available to you, nothing will happen until you turn on the switch. If you are afraid that your life, health, and/or happiness will be unbearably worse, turn on the switch that connects you with the 24/7 power source available to us all.

The less time you devote to being afraid the more time you spend in a positive, spiritual mindset, and the better off you'll be.

I regret every squandered moment I spent being scared. Life is a lot better now that I've learned that whatever happens, no matter how ominous it seems, I'll be able to cope, thanks to the faith-based airwaves just waiting for me to turn the switch.

5. REALIGNMENT/ATTITUDE ADJUSTMENT. Several years ago I wrote an article for a women's magazine about the trouble many adults have changing the way they see themselves. Back then, I focused on how hard it is for women whose self image had been formed when they were young and awkward, to see the beauty that was so obvious to others once they had blossomed. I wrote about three women: a once-overweight woman who now wears a size 6, but still sees nonexistent flabby thighs or a thick waist; an attractive, intelligent lawyer who wore braces as an adult to straighten crooked teeth, and still finds it hard to believe that she has a lovely smile; and a pretty woman who can't see her own beauty because of the horror of high school acne, eyeglasses and braces. The pimples and the braces are gone, and contacts have replaced the glasses, but this very attractive woman will never recognize herself as the object of beauty that others see.

Thanks to journalistic professional objectivity, I thought these women were silly to cling to useless and invalid images of themselves. Today, I can better understand the indelible power of the past. Wishing for the former me wasn't a wise use of my time. Proverbs 13:12 could have succinctly taught me that *Hope deferred makes the heart sick.*

I still think of myself as a 5' 6" athletically built woman who is independent, competitive, impatient, and achievement orient-ed. In my mind's eye, I have firm muscles and my ice skates and riding boots are within arm's reach. In reality, the person I am today is three feet tall and, having spent too many years in a wheelchair, my once-muscular body is far more flabby than firm.

One of my personal heroes is a journalist in Providence, Rhode Island named Brian Dickerson. He was nominated for the Pulitzer Prize for his weekly columns in The Providence Journal-Bulletin. Dickerson has ALS, or Lou Gehrig's disease, and writes with only the middle finger of his left hand, which is one of the few parts of his body that still moves. It takes him about 15 hours to compose his column, which he writes with the help of his developed-for-the-disabled computer.

This Harvard-educated former New York Times staffer once observed: "One of the many truths about a serious illness, I've learned, is that it utterly transforms the way one regards the world. Perspective is drastically, permanently altered." For people with physical challenges, our perspective of ourselves changes slowly, painfully, and reluctantly. Perhaps it's because we each have a window of opportunity, when we are young, through which our vision of self is captured. That "photo op," as it were, remains relatively static and impervious to reality as we age. In the corners of their minds, bald men still have hair; slim women still see imaginary unsightly rolls of fat. Those of us in wheelchairs still "see" ourselves as able to walk and stand tall, especially in our dreams.

Many years ago, a wise and gracious woman comforted me when I was feeling overwhelmed by the prospect of raising two sons on my own. I was bemoaning the fact that I had no brother, uncle or father to support me when it came to sharing my values on how to help boys grow into men. This elegant widow had raised two charming and accomplished sons by herself. She told me that, now that her boys were adults, it was easy for her to objectively see which lessons had and had not been important. As solemnly as if she were sharing the formula for nuclear fission she said, "The most important skill you can give your sons is the ability to be fluid. They need to know that in school, in sports, in life, things will never stay the same. Their world will go through many changes, and as long as they can bend, they will never break. And the easier it is for them to bend, the easier it will be for them to avoid rigidity and adapt to whatever the future holds."

I like to think that I managed to follow her advice and subtly passed on that skill to my sons, for they have certainly handled divorce, death, and even my disability with remarkable skill and maturity. I, however, have not. Kicking and screaming (figuratively), I have clutched that old type-A Wonder-Woman self-image close to my heart, even after it no longer made any sense at all. Circumstances have pried away that out-of-date image, finger by rigid finger and a new Marilyn is slowly coming into view. I am short, flabby, and reduced to all-too-frequently being forced to ask other people for help. But that's okay, because, like it or not, the person I am is no longer defined by what I do physically or by how I look.

It has taken me a long time to get to the point where I could identify with Charles L. Allen's words: "I had to forget about useless 'if only's' . . . I had to grasp the shining truth that those of us confined to beds or wheelchairs or solitary rooms still possess gifts of the highest order. We can show love. We can display humor, courage, friendliness, Godliness, unencumbered by the demands placed on the able-bodied."

And just because I'm a different me doesn't mean I'm a less valuable me. It has taken 15 years of fighting my physical failings to accept the validity of that sentence. I have a redesigned life now, one with different challenges, new goals, and new rewards. And one of my ambitions is to accept, with as much grace as I can muster, the advice of dancer/model/actress Dayle Haddon: "What is important is that you never give up. Keep recreating who you are, and you'll find that every moment has something to offer."

6. UNEXPECTED BLESSINGS. If you have to live in a wheelchair, it helps to be a writer. Fortunately for me, I can still earn a living, albeit vastly reduced, without the use of my legs. And because I love the written word, my mind can take me places neither my legs nor my wheelchair can. So I continue to learn and learn and learn. Kind people, loving friends, and my belief system ease the struggle, and I continue to believe that there's a reason why the life I once took completely for granted is now so far beyond my shaky grasp.

Perhaps my illness was sent to me so that I could learn a different way of looking at life, one that I was in too much of a hurry to truly appreciate. There's a lesson here somewhere, I know. These days, my goal is to study hard enough, long enough, diligently enough, until I earn my doctorate in disability. Then I want to graduate into a freer state of mind, full of uncoerced higher learning. And I want to do so – regardless of the problems I face – with an endless capacity for unhandicapped happiness. In other words, I want to learn whatever I'm meant to learn from this experience so that I can be as productively evolved as possible. And then, once I "get it" (As Dr. Phil would say), accept my situation with a smile rather than a struggle.

~11~

YOU ARE NOT ALONE

A wheelchair dependent life does include certain social restrictions, which means, like it or not, you'll probably spend more time alone than you would prefer. But the first lesson a disabled person learns is that there's a world of difference between being alone and being lonely. I have learned that restructuring my support system was actually, a pretty rewarding experience. Frame of mind, attitude, and choice are key elements.

To begin with, the most helpful frame of mind is one that allows you to focus on the wonderful opportunities in your current situation. The people who have the hardest time accepting an altered life are those who view their circumstances only as some form of unredeemable loss or defeat. To turn around this counterproductive pattern, some people practice positive thinking, others rely on their religious beliefs, and some focus on spirituality.

Whatever path you choose, the process is the same. It boils down to accepting that even though your life may not be the one you thought you would have, God still has plans for you. Your job is to keep your mind and heart in a receptive state to accept the "altered blessings" that are headed your way.

When I worked at a newspaper in London, a woman I

admired told me that her family's Greek Orthodox belief helped her get through tough times that would have pulverized her non-believing peers. "We believe that whenever life takes something away, God replaces it with something better. Setbacks aren't an end. They just open up a way for God to guide us to something even better," she told me.

When it comes to attitude, nothing is more helpful than a reliable support group. You might prefer attending meetings of people who share your reality and can relate to the challenges you face. Spinal cord injury, multiple sclerosis, ALS, muscular dystrophy, cerebral palsy and numerous other conditions have local and national support organizations. You can call your local office or check their website for information and help.

Perhaps because I'm not much of a joiner, I fashioned my own support group from old friends and new acquaintances. As they did for me, some wonderful people will come into your life as paid aides. Others, including neighbors and friends, will arrive as willing, charitable helpers. Their bodies may not experience the aches and challenges that your does, but the company and caring hearts make your burden easier to bear.

There are, of course, a variety of choices to make regarding your personalized form of "assisted living." You might want to live with others or have someone live with you. You might choose to hire someone for a set number of hours each week to help maintain a comfortable lifestyle. Or you might choose to live on your own for as long as possible. This is just one of many decisions that you need to make on your own, preferably after lots of prayer and quiet introspection. This is not the time to let well-meaning, able-bodied people tell you what to do.

When I could still drive (in my former car with overhead wheelchair storage lift), I enjoyed a unique and rewarding relationship with two neighborhood adolescent girls. Our friendship began when I bought Girl Scout cookies from them, and over the years it gradually progressed to the point where they would spend one night each weekend sleeping happily on my sofa bed. We made an arrangement that for every hour they spent helping me with household challenges (such as decorating for Christmas, Easter, Fourth of July, etc. or addressing Christmas card envelopes), I would reciprocate by spending an equal amount of time with them at the Mall or at an age-appropriate movie. They were delighted to be needed and treated like responsible adults, and their overworked moms were pleased to be relieved of weekend trips to the mall. I was tickled pink to have a win-win situation that allowed me to simultaneously give and receive.

The important thing to remember is that when you take responsibility for carving out the lifestyle you want, good things happen. Proactively managing a challenging situation automatically increases your self-esteem as well as your ability to accomplish goals.

Years ago, I was caught in a particularly unpleasant situation when someone who was supposed to retrieve me from their home's handicap inaccessible bathroom inadvertently forgot to do so. Stuck alone in a small room and unable to get myself out, I had no choice but to wait. My initial reaction was to feel sorry for myself, to blame my uncooperative body, rail inwardly at the healthy but forgetful people who had failed to retrieve me. I watched the minutes slowly tick by before finding a book that had previously escaped my notice. Determined to make the best of a bad situation, I opened the book and began to read. I quickly forgot about my ridiculous predicament and began to enjoy the words that were before me.

I may not have mentioned earlier that I attended UCLA back

when it held the national NCAA Championship for an unheard-of record of ten years. Our quietly devout basketball coach, John Wooden, was considered a man of mythic proportions on campus, and when we students happened to see him in the cafeteria or at the bookstore, it was a big deal. He was always unfailingly polite, even to those of us who had never learned how to dribble. The book I serendipitously found in that bathroom included a story about his philosophy, and ever since that frustrating day I've used it as my own personal pick-me-up motto.

Wooden wasn't writing about handicapped bodies nor was he speaking specifically to disabled people, but his words have helped me countless times and I hope they resonate with you as well. Quite simply, Coach Wooden urged all of us to remember that we must never let what we can't do stop us from doing what we can. Remembering Coach Wooden's advice will make whatever challenges you face in this lifetime – physical or otherwise – a lot easier to bear.

∿12∿

HEROES

All too often a disability is viewed as a perfect excuse to take a vacation from achievement. After all, even able bodied people find making dreams come true a daunting challenge. That is why I pay attention to stories about inspiring men and women who refuse to take the easy way out simply because their bodies have let them down. I would like to share with you my favorite stories about inspiring people who have accepted their disability and rejected the idea that they can no longer live a fulfilling life.

• **Carolyn Stern** is one of only a dozen or so deaf doctors in the United States. She practices medicine in Rochester, New York, home to the 1200-student National Technical Institute for the Deaf. This technical college for the non-hearing has given Rochester the largest non-hearing population per capita in the nation (90,000 of the city's 350,000). Doctor Stern's office has flashing lights to let patients know when someone is about to enter their examination room and her staff is fluent in sign language.

Teased mercilessly when she started public school at age five, Stern now understands why her parents refused to send her to a deaf school. They wanted her to be part of mainstream life. One consequence of her childhood sense of isolation was her high academic achievements and her determination to play the violin. Stern's mother had contracted German measles during her pregnancy, which resulted in Carolyn's limited ability to hear and gradual deafness. By the time Stern went to college, she knew that her future lay in medicine. She graduated cum laude in 1986 from Northwestern University Medical School where she wore a microphone that transmitted lectures into her hearing aids. The school provided a sign language interpreter to help her participate in class discussions. Stern's mettle was tested when the school stopped providing interpreters because of budget constraints. She sued and after a two-year legal battle, the suit was settled in her favor.

Stern's residency at Lutheran General Hospital in Park Ridge, Illinois coincided with further loss of hearing, which she interpreted as a sign that she was meant to work with the deaf community. Stern finally received a cochlear implant and married a hearing man who had had deaf parents. Now the mother of three, Stern uses a super charged stethoscope on her patients and uses her own loss of hearing to help her be a better doctor to patients who would otherwise be unable to share information with a hearing physician.

• **Tim Lefens,** an abstract painter, learned that he had retinitis pigmentosa in 1989. Although he had not been financially successful as an artist, and supported himself with tree-trimming jobs, he worried that his art life was coming to an untimely end.

Around the year 1994, he visited the Matheny School and Hospital for the Developmentally Disabled in Peapack, New Jersey, where most students are unable to talk or even communicate with sign language. At the time, Lefens was still able to see faces perfectly and he saw a sense of desperation. He decided to find a way for wheelchair-confined people to communicate using art therapy. Lefens joined the staff at Matheny and developed a method for a wheelchair-bound artist to direct a laser attached to a hat to transmit a signal to an able-bodied person, who would then apply the paint. Lefens knows that at some point he will be totally blind, but in the meantime has done much to help those who would otherwise not be able to paint. He is founder of the nonprofit Artistic Realization Technologies, which has now spread to Virginia, Florida, and California

• **Bev Kearney** of the University of Texas in Austin has long been considered one of America's top track and field coaches. She has mentored six Olympic medalists and coached her teams to five national championships. These days, however, she is no longer able to walk because of a car accident that killed two friends and left her paralyzed below the knees. Kearney's goal is to eventually walk unaided. Her determination imparts a strong message of hope to student athletes not only at the University of Texas, but to the athletic world.

• **Katherine Sherwood** was teaching graduate painting classes at University of California at Berkeley until she suffered a massive cerebral hemorrhage in 1997. A successful artist whose abstract works hung in galleries and museums on the East and West coasts of America, Sherwood's entire right side was paralyzed, and she lost her ability to speak. She thought she would never teach art again. After she relearned how to walk and talk, Sherwood began painting with her left hand. The result was a reinvigorated career. Speech therapy helped her overcome partial tongue paralysis and six months of physical therapy helped her learn how to walk again using a cane. Her left-handed canvases using acrylic paints in lighter colors now sell in the $20,000 range, about three times what the former right-handed oils did.

• **Laura Hillenbrand's** book, _Seabiscuit: An American Legend_ spent more than 80 weeks on the New York Times bestseller list and was turned into an award-winning movie. But what most people don't know is that the author suffers from chronic fatigue syndrome (CFS) and wrote the book during times of severe illness. A mysterious illness that allows people to look normal although they feel terrible, CFS is disabling in its own way. Hillenbrand told one reviewer that while most people think chronic fatigue syndrome means not having enough energy to get out of the house, it can actually mean feeling as if there isn't enough energy to even breathe. It was Hillenbrand's struggle with the disease that led her to recognize the heroism in Seabiscuit's story. A book about a small horse, an unconventional jockey, and a grieving owner represented just the sort of triumph over adversity that would appeal to an author with health challenges. Hillenbrand's fight against her body's sickness just may have been the unknown factor that gave her the strength to finish her inspiring book. Too ill to lead a normal life, she channeled all her strength into the words in a wildly successful book. After having been forced to drop out of the world for years, her illness gave her the gift of a world with unlimited boundaries.

• **Christopher Reeve** suffered a horrific accident in Culpeper, Virginia that destroyed his motor and sensory function. Since that time in May 1995, he has worked tirelessly to give hope to countless people like me who have been told that physiological improvement simply is not possible. If you are able-bodied, imagine how those of us with disabilities reacted when Reeve, who is more disabled than most paralyzed people, proved the physicians wrong. They had told him that he would never regain movement or feeling below the shoulders. After a demanding regimen of consistent exercises on an electrical-stimulation stationary bike, by 2001 he could consciously initiate small movements in his arms and legs. By 2004, he had regained feeling in 70% of his body.

Reeve makes no secret that he thinks both doctors and scientists need to eliminate the word "impossible" from their vocabularies. I agree. Back in 1998, when I reviewed Reeve's first book, <u>Still Me</u> for the Palm Beach Post, I had been a wheelchair user for several years. Like Reeve, I lost my ability to walk at age 42. I had been an active, athletic woman and adapting to my disability has been a life-altering challenge. Reading Reeve's eerily similar struggle, along with his conflicted reaction to a new reality, had a profound effect on my psyche.

Reeve wrote, "People often ask me what it's like to have sustained a spinal cord injury and be confined to a wheelchair. Apart from all the medical complications, I would say the worst part of it is leaving the physical world – having had to make the transition from participant to observer long before I would have expected . . . To have it all change at age 42 is devastating. As much as I remind myself that being is more important than doing. That the quality of relationships is the key to happiness, I'm actually putting on a brave face. I do believe those things are true, but I miss freedom, spontaneity, action, and adventure more than I can say.

What solidified my admiration for Reeve was what he decided to do with his life after he became paralyzed. Instead of just accepting the conventional medical wisdom that paralysis is forever, Reeve established The Christopher Reeve Paralysis Foundation, and began enlisting the world's leading scientists, researchers, and physicians to unlock the secrets of the spinal cord and neurological disorders.

"Research crosses all the barriers -- we're thinking as aggressively as we possibly can. We will not be complacent. We will not take no for an answer. If someone says that they can't do something, we want to know why, and then we want to move the field forward as rapidly possible."

Reeve doesn't just push others; he has worked unceasingly on his own rehabilitation. Using a stationary bicycle, electrical muscular stimulator, special treadmill and pool therapy, he has managed to increase his bone density and strength. The experts who had told him his physical condition could not improve were wrong. The man who was told that he would never feel or move his extremities can now do a little of both.

He told me "Since about 2000 I have kept my training time the same at 45 minutes at 48 rpm. In that time I cover eight miles and get my heart rate from 57 to 98. I try to do it at least two or three times per week, usually on Monday, Wednesday, and Friday mornings."

Last year he was honored by the prestigious Lasker Foundation for "heroic advocacy for medical research in general and victims for disabilities". Science is fueled by funding, and The Christopher Reeve Paralysis Foundation now offers more than 13 million dollars in grants each year. More than anyone else, Reeve has made it his personal quest to transform medical research. And that is why he is my personal superhero.

When I read Still Me, and his second book Nothing Is Impossible, Reeve's battle with an altered world and his uncooperative body resonates with painful familiarity. But his struggle to breathe and his reliance on a ventilator left me totally amazed. I can only imagine what it would be like to listen to each and every inhalation. Last year he underwent a laparoscopic procedure at Case Western Reserve University in Cleveland, Ohio, to insert a pacemaker that causes the diaphragm to contract.

Instead of needing to be continually connected to the ventilator and the whooshing noise it makes, Reeve can now breathe off the ventilator as much as 20 hours a day.

Reeve's passionate quest to transform medicine and eliminate paralysis is not without its critics. Some researchers feel that he is too impatient and unjustly willing to side step normal testing procedures. And even a small number of the people most likely to benefit from his foundation's research question his optimistic belief that paralysis doesn't have to be permanent. Reeve scoffs at the accusation that he is "in denial."

It is no secret that Christopher Reeve is comfortable using his celebrity as a magnet for attracting donations, creating political awareness, and generating media attention. Since I know what paralysis does to a person's soul, I remain in awe of how this remarkable, highly intelligent, and well-educated man lives his day-to-day life. When there are no television cameras, black tie award dinners, or journalists hanging on his every word, how does he maintain his emotional equilibrium, sense of humor, and faith in a brighter tomorrow? When I asked he said, "I've learned to ignore my moods because I've learned that whatever mood I'm in at any given moment will change before too long. And I accept that for even being in a good mood. Of course, I appreciate being in a good mood a great deal, but you can expect setbacks, and expect to be feeling better one day and not at all well the next day. It's really just a question of putting it in perspective."

My personal understanding of paralysis tells me that no amount of hired help or medically open-minded insurance policies can ever totally eliminate the black clouds of negativity that rise to the surface when you least expect them, or not emotionally prepared to deal with them. It is particularly challenging when your dreams at night never include a wheelchair. I dance, Reeve skis, we both sail over fences on horseback, and then we wake up each morning to cope once again with uncooperative limbs that ignore the signals from our brains. When we sleep, we run, hop in and out of cars, climb stairs, and stretch effortlessly to grasp items just out of reach. But when we awaken, we are deeply dependent people who need someone else to help us get out of bed, get dressed and groomed, prepare our food, bathe, and on, and on, and on.

The X factor in Reeve's remarkable display of resilience is the love and support he receives from his wife, actress Dana Morosini Reeve, and his three children. Matthew, age 23 is a documentary filmmaker who lives in England. Daughter Alexandra is the captain of the Yale Polo team (their mother is Gae Exton); Christopher and Dana's son, Will is eleven years old. Reeve once worried that his severe injuries would destroy his family or "ruin everybody's life," but these days his family is closer than ever before.

He said, "I've had to learn that what kids want is for you to notice their accomplishments, go to their games, their recitals, and be aware of what is important to them even if you can't actively participate in the traditional way." *

I, too, am lucky enough to not be alone during my physical and emotional wrestling match with paralysis. Seven years ago I met a remarkable man who, much like Dana Reeve, did not see a partner with paralysis as an impediment to a happy and rewarding life. I was in a wheelchair when Tony and I met and fell in love, when he proposed, and when we were married in 1998. Tony never complains, but it can't be a walk in the park to juggle the challenging emotional and physical demands of living with a disabled spouse. When our friends want to tease Tony or me about his ever-generous attentiveness, they just good-naturedly refer to him as Saint Anthony. . .

People with mobility challenges have the potential to serve as quiet, unexpected role models to our able-bodied friends. Among other lessons, the past twenty years have taught me that while physical possibilities may be curtailed by circumstance, emotional ones are simply a matter of choice. How each of us chooses to think, behave, and love — in or out of a wheelchair – will be our legacy; and the simple act of acknowledging that possibility is a reminder that each of our lives contain the capacity for boundless blessings.

Editor's note: "We regret that Christopher Reeve died unexpectedly just as this book was being printed. We share the sadness of his family and friends. May God bless them, and may God bless the memory of this remarkable man."

SUGGESTED READING

Waist-High In The World by Nancy Mairs (Beacon Press, 1996, $20)

For years now, essayist Nancy Mairs has lived in a wheelchair due to the progression of her multiple sclerosis. From her distinctive perspective, she has written provocatively, courageously and to great acclaim about marriage, faith, art, and illness

Still Me by Christopher Reeve (Random House, 1998, $25.00)

This New York Times best-selling autobiography takes the reader through Christopher Reeve's life from childhood to post-accident life. He pointedly shares the journey he has made and analyzes the family relationships that influenced both his personal and professional life. This touching story of how one man and his family adapted to a traumatic turn of events offers a great roadmap for anyone baffled by the challenge of coping with a disability.

Nothing Is Impossible by Christopher Reeve (Random House, 2002, $19.95)

Christopher Reeve has mastered the art of turning the impossible into the inevitable. In his second book, the author shows that we are all capable of overcoming seemingly insurmountable hardships. He interweaves anecdotes from his own life with excerpts from speeches and interviews he has given. The book includes evocative photos taken by his son Matthew.

Moving Violations by John Hockenberry (Hyperion, 1995, $24.95)

This is one of the most entertaining, provocative, unexpected, outspoken, and occasionally outrageous books in recent memory. It is a story of obstacles – physical, emotional, and psychic – overcome again, and again, and again by a journalist confined to a wheelchair since the age of 18.

My Soul Purpose by Heidi von Beltz with Peter Copeland
(Random House, 1996, $24.00)

At 25, Heidi von Beltz was an actress, model, and aspiring movie producer on Hollywood's fast track to success. Tall and beautiful, she was also a professional skier and stuntwoman. On June 25, 1980, on the set of the movie "The Cannonball Run," a chase scene Heidi was filming went wrong, and the tiny sports car she was riding in crashed head-on into a van. Doctors pronounced her paralyzed from the neck down and advised that she prepare for a miserable, brief life best spent in an institution. But Heidi looked deep inside her soul and found the spiritual key to healing: the awareness of a greater power that anyone can access.

Blindsided: Living a Life Above Illness by Richard Cohen
(Harpercollins, 2004)

Thirty years ago producer/journalist Richard Cohen was diagnosed with MS. Since that time he has married television personality Meredith Vieira, fathered three children, tailored his career to his physical limitations, and coped with colon cancer. This frank memoir tells how Cohen and his wife have coped with the ever-present shadow of illness without losing their love for each other, their determination, or their respective sense of humor. Both Cohen's father and grandmother had MS and he writes pointedly of his concern for the couple's three adolescent children. This is a moving and inspiring story of how one couple's optimism and affection has helped them come face to face with health challenges.

Climbing Higher by Montel Williams (New American Library, 2004 $25.95)

Montel Williams was first struck with symptoms of MS in

1979. Two decades later, he received a clear diagnosis, and set about restructuring his life. As a celebrity, he informed his family and friends, went public with the news, and then made up his mind to live the most productive life possible while at the same time becoming a public fundraiser and spokesperson for the disease. This deeply personal memoir is inspiring, motivating, and remarkably honest, not only about his physical challenges, but about the emotional repercussions of coping with a challenging disease.

___A Whole New Life___ by Reynolds Price (Athanaeum Press, 1994, $20.00)

Beyond the particulars of pain and paraplegia, larger concerns surface here, including a determination to reconnect with the human interaction that is so much a part of this writer's much-loved work, the gratitude he feels toward his friends and some of his doctors, the return to his prolific work, and the "now appalling, now astonishing grace of God."

___Beyond MS___ by Nancy A. Bent (Random House, 1995, $25.00)

In 1976, Nancy A. Bent was told by medical specialists that she had multiple sclerosis a degenerative disease that would not go away. Refusing to accept this negative way of life, her search for another option led her to a new mode of treatment. This engaging book is the personal story of Nancy's remarkable recovery from multiple sclerosis and her unique journey of mental images, which even went beyond MS to increased health and vitality.

___GUIDEPOSTS MAGAZINE___ (www.guideposts.com)

This small non-denominational monthly magazine is full of inspirational and uplifting first-person stories. I keep a copy with me at all times because I simply never know when I might need a mini-spiritual pick-me-up.

DESERT MINISTRIES INCORPORATED

Desert Ministries is a non-profit corporation devoted to the development of helpful materials for use by those in special need. It provides books and booklets for clergy and for laity on a variety of subjects. Information on other publications will be sent upon request. A sample packet will be sent without charge if you ask.

Recent publications include: *When You Lose Someone You Love, How to Help an Alcoholic, Christ Will See You Through, God's Promises and My Needs, You Now Have Custody of You, When Alzheimer's Strikes, When A Child Dies, A Journey Through Cancer,* and more.

Desert Ministries, Inc.
P.O. Box 747
Matthews, North Carolina 28106-0747

wwww.desmin.org

APPENDIX
WHEELCHAIR FOUNDATION

The heart-warming testimony you have just read is happening to millions of people all over the world. Some lose the ability to walk because of accidents, some diseases, war, land-mines, old age, etc. It is estimated that 100-150 million people with physical disabilities worldwide need wheelchairs.

Someone decided to do something about this terrible situation and in June of 2000, Ken Behring, a philanthropist, formed the Wheelchair Foundation.

The Wheelchair Foundation's mission is to lead an international effort to create awareness of the needs and abilities of people with physical disabilities, to promote the joy of giving, create global friendship, and to deliver a wheelchair to every child, teen and adult in the world who needs one, but cannot afford one. For these people, the Wheelchair Foundation delivers Hope, Mobility and Freedom.

There are people like Marilyn but millions of others who have no insurance or no means to purchase a wheelchair—that's where the Wheelchair Foundation comes in. As of September of 2004, the Wheelchair Foundation had delivered close to 300,000 free wheelchairs to people without mobility in 130 countries and right here at home.

You can be a part of the mission of the Wheelchair Foundation with only a $75 tax-deductible donation (per wheelchair). That's right! Only $75 can give someone a new manual wheelchair, that if purchased individually would cost between $375 to $500. The Wheelchair Foundation purchases and delivers more than 10,000 wheelchairs per month all over the world.

To be involved is very easy - just contact me and let me know how many wheelchairs you'd like to donate and within months we will send you photos of the people whose life you changed. When you donate, please refer to this book. Thank you.

Jack Drury, President
Southeast Region
WHEELCHAIR FOUNDATION
2800 E. Commercial Blvd., Suite 207
Fort Lauderdale, Florida 33308
954-776-0722
Email: WheelsFlorida@aol.com
Website: www.wheelchairfoundation.org